Be a Buddy, No

MW00886922

By Loverly Sheridan

Edited by: Jessica Dylan Winter

Illustrated by MacKenzie Rattray

All rights reserved to the publisher, author and illustrator. No part of this publication may be reproduced or stored in a retrieval system, or transmitted in any form or by any means electronic, mechanical, photocopying, recording or otherwise, without permission from all of the above mentioned.

Copyright © 2012 Loverly Sheridan
All rights reserved.
ISBN-13: 978-1511531191
ISBN-10: 1511531193

Dedication

For Donnalyn Wittman, my childhood friend, my buddy.
And for my beloved Matthew, Tyler, Jahdez, Jada, Noah,
Judah, Christian,Tarik, Faith and Kaya.
May you always be a Buddy.

Acknowledgement

Children bully or are bullied by others in many different ways. Most of it starts at a very early age when they are unable to understand the effects and consequences of their actions, and are simply expressing their feelings and frustrations, or simply succumbing to peer pressure.

There are many factors which influence bullying, and although there isn't one solution to stop it, we can help curb it by speaking to our children about being more compassionate, tolerant and embracive of others. We can teach them about team building, sharing, caring and how to use their words effectively. Most importantly, because children learn more by our example, as parents, it's important in our everyday lives to exercise those same practices with others, so they can learn first-hand what it means to be a buddy and not a bully.

I would like to thank my 'anti - bully' team (Shawn, Caroli, Cecilia, Mackenzie, Lauren, Jessica, Melanie, Delane and Daleon) who shared in my vision to write and create a story to help teach children the importance of being a friend and a leader. I believe that if we provide our children with the right tools and teach them like Kate in the story to be kind to others, and lead by example, then we will help in making this world a much better place.

Dear Buddy: Please sign this book and take the pledge.

My name is: _____

Pledge: **'I am a Buddy, Not a bully!'**

Tomorrow is the first day of school.

Kate is so excited, she can't sleep!

"I can't wait to meet my

new teacher and friends,"

Kate said to her mother.

"Please try to get some sleep.

Tomorrow is a big day and

you do not want to be tired,"

said Kate's mother.

Kate lay in bed staring at the ceiling.

1

She wondered how many kids would be in her class.

She wondered if her experience at the new school would be anything like homeschool in Paris.

Kate had been homeschooled since she was three years old.

Being in a regular school was going to be new for her.

As the bright morning sun shone through the window, Kate jumped out of bed.

She rushed to brush her teeth and dressed herself in her new school uniform.

"I'm all ready to go!" she shouted.

"Not so fast, little lady. Don't forget to say your prayers and eat your breakfast,"

said mother.

Kate closed her eyes and prayed she would have the best first day at school.

She quickly ate her breakfast and rushed out the front door to wait for

the big yellow school bus.

This was Kate's first time taking the bus and she couldn't wait to ride in it.

She was so excited that she forgot to kiss her mother goodbye.

"Aren't you forgetting something?" mother asked as she followed

Kate to the bus.

"I'm sorry, mom. I'm just so excited to get to school to meet

all my new friends,"

Kate said with wonder. She gave her mom a big hug.

Kate hopped onto the bus and sat in the first window seat she could find.

She looked out the window and waved goodbye to her mother as the

lemon yellow transporter carried her away.

At the next stop, a few kids were lined up waiting for their turn to get onboard.

There was a little boy crying aloud. He did not want to get onto the bus.

His mother walked him onboard as she tried to comfort him.

She looked around for an empty seat and saw there was one next to Kate.

"It's okay, Jesse. You will have the best first day of school ever,"

said his mother as she sat him down next to Kate.

Jesse kept crying as his mother walked away.

SCHOOL BUS

Two kids, Mason and Benny, were sitting behind Jesse and Kate.

As the bus drove off, they started to make funny sounds.

They also began to laugh loudly. "What a baby!" Benny shouted.

"I want my mommy," Mason teased in a squeaky voice.

They kept making fun of Jesse while laughing.

This made Jesse very sad and he cried even more.

Kate felt sorry for Jesse. She wanted to say something to the boys,

but she was scared.

"What if they tease me, too?" she thought to herself.

She decided she would try to cheer up Jesse.

She wanted him to be excited about his first day of school, just like she was.

"Hi, my name is Kate. I'm in the first grade.

What grade are you in?" Kate said to Jesse.

Jesse lowered his head and kept crying.

Kate pulled out a blank sticker pad from her book bag.

"Hey, maybe we can write our names on these stickers and stick them

on our shirts so everyone will know our names," she said.

Jesse shrugged his shoulders. "Okay," he said.

As the bus pulled up to the school, the kids began rushing off of it to get

 to their classrooms.

But not Jesse! He began crying again and would not get off the bus.

As Mason and Benny walked passed him,

they made funny faces and called him a baby.

"Come on Jesse, you can do it," Kate said.

"I'll walk with you to your class if you'd like."

Jesse reached his hand out towards Kate and walked with her off the bus.

As they walked to Jesse's classroom, Kate realized she and Jesse were assigned to the same class.

"Look! We are in the same class!" Kate said as she jumped up and down.

Jesse was also excited about this. He felt a lot more relaxed.

They were greeted by their new teacher, Mrs. Phillips, when they

entered the classroom.

Their classroom name tags were placed nicely at their individual desks.

There were three big tables in the classroom with boys and

girls sitting around them.

Kate counted the number of children around each table.

There were more boys than girls.

As she looked around, she saw that Mason and Benny were also in the class.

"Oh no! I hope they don't tease Jesse anymore," she thought to herself.

Mrs. Phillips then began to read aloud the class rules.

The first rule on her paper read, "NO BULLYING AND NO TEASING."

Kate and Jesse stared at each other. Should they tell their teacher what

happened on the bus?

Kate's mother always told her to speak with a teacher

or another adult if someone teased her.

She decided she wouldn't interrupt Mrs. Phillips while she continued

reading through the rules.

She would tell her about what happened on the bus later in the day.

Jesse remained quiet because he was too scared to say anything.

At recess, all the kids ran outside to play.

Kate and Jesse were so excited about playing outside that they forgot about speaking with Mrs. Phillips.

Kate met Jesse on the playground. They had fun playing and doing push-ups with their new friends.

"Jesse, would you like to race to the water fountain?" Kate asked.

"You bet!" said Jesse. And off they ran together.

Just before they reached the water fountain, Kate saw a little boy crying

in the corner behind the wall.

It was Mason, one of the boys who teased Jesse on the bus.

"Look, Jesse, it's Mason. He's crying. Something is wrong,"

Kate said anxiously. "Let's help him."

Jessie hesitated, "I don't know, maybe we shouldn't," he said,

"Mason may be mean to me again, and why should I help him?

He was not very nice to me!"

"Well, my mom always says that I should lead by example." Kate said

Maybe we should show him what it means to be kind to others, right?

"Okay, you're right. But you ask him," said Jesse.

Kate slowly walked up to Mason. "What's wrong?" she asked.

"Leave me alone!" Mason screamed as he buried his head in his knees.

"Maybe I can help," she said.

"No, you can't! Girls cannot do push-ups!" Mason shouted.

"What do you mean?" asked Kate.

Mason slowly lifted his head. Tears were flowing down his cheeks.

"Jason and his friends keep laughing at me.

They said I look silly doing push-ups and

that I can't do them very well," said Mason.

"It's okay," Kate said. "I didn't know how to do push-ups either,

but my dad showed me.

I practiced a little bit every day

unitil I figured it out. I can show you if you want."

"Whoa! I thought girls couldn't do push-ups," said Mason.

"This is amazing!"

Kate showed Mason a trick her dad taught her.

This trick made the push-ups a lot easier for her.

"Cross your legs *(feet)* and remain on your knees.

Make sure your legs *(feet)* are not touching the ground.

Then place your hands on the ground

and push your upper body up and down like this,"

she instructed as Mason and Jesse looked on.

"WOW! This is so much easier," Mason shouted.

Then he gave it a try. It was a bit difficult at first.

He wanted to give up.

Jessie stepped in and said, "Maybe you can first practice it with your feet on the ground and once you get better, you can try it with your feet off the ground."

"That's a great idea. Thanks Jessie!" Mason said.

"I can do it! I can do it!" Mason said excitedly.

"Don't get too excited just yet, you must practise a little more at home and then you will be great," Jessie said.

"I can't wait to show Jason and his friends how well I can

do push-ups tomorrow," Mason said.

"Thank you for helping me with my push-ups, Kate and Jesse,"

said Mason.

"You both are so much fun! Can we be friends?

I can show you some cool things too," Mason said.

"Sure! I love learning new things," Kate said. "But first I think you must apologize to Jesse for teasing him on the bus. You really hurt his feelings."

Jesse lowered his head and said shyly,

"Yes, you did hurt my feelings, Mason. It made me sad."

"I'm sorry Jesse. I didn't mean to hurt your feelings." Mason said.

"I was just trying to be cool by following

 what my friend Benny was doing. That was silly of me."

"It's okay. I forgive you," Jesse said.

"Great! Now we can all be friends and

learn new things from each other," said Kate.

"Let's all race back to class. Catch me if you can!"

Kate yelled as she ran off with both boys chasing behind her.

When the big yellow school bus came to pick up the kids after school, Jesse, Mason and Kate all sat together.

They talked about their fun day at school and the new things they had learned.

Kate was the first one to be dropped off.

Her mother was waiting for her outside and couldn't wait to hear

about her day.

"So, tell me all about your big day!" Kate's mother said

with a huge smile.

"It was the best day! I met new friends and I like my new teacher.

But I learned an important lesson today."

"Oh? What's that?" asked mother.

"To always be a buddy, not a bully. You make more friends that way and you learn new things, too!" said Kate confidently.

"Yes, my dear, you are right!" mother said as she hugged Kate tightly.

Let's repeat the Pledge!

Hey Buddy! Here are a few questions for you to answer.

Have fun learning about you!

Have you ever been bullied?

_____

Why were you bullied?

_____

How did it make you feel?

_____

How did you respond to your bully?

_____

After reading this book, how will you respond next time?

_____

_____

Have you witnessed someone being bullied?

_____

What did you do?

_____

After reading his book, how will you respond next time?

_____

_____

_____

Biography

Loverly Sheridan is a native of Saint Lucia, an island which is located in the Eastern Caribbean Sea. As an author and globetrotter, Loverly finds great enjoyment in telling stories which uplift and empower people to be inspired to live their best. Through the translation of her experiences, she encourages people to live in peace and harmony with each other. This is her third children's book, of which all are geared towards empowering children to embrace their uniqueness and that of others. Loverly is a proud mother to a happy and loving six-year old son named Matthew-Anthony.

20852637R00024

Made in the USA
San Bernardino, CA
26 April 2015